Book 1
Malware
By Solis Tech

&

Book 2
Human-Computer Interaction
By Solis Tech

Book 1
Malware
By Solis Tech

Malware Detection & Threats Made Easy!

Malware: Malware Detection & Threats Made Easy!

Table of Contents

Introduction

I want to thank you and congratulate you for purchasing the book, *"Malware: Malware Detection & Threats Made Easy!"*.

This book contains proven steps and strategies on how to avoid, detect and remove malware.

Malware creators are very creative, employing both technical and social means to spread malware. Simply installing antivirus software is no longer enough. This book explains how malware spreads in order to arm the reader with information on how to manage its threat.

Thanks again for purchasing this book, I hope you enjoy it!

Chapter 1 – Malware

Computers are inherently dumb. They can accept and input data, can process it at high-speed, and can return the results almost instantly. However, users need to tell the computer what to do in the form of codes. We call these codes programs, applications, scripts or software, but they are essentially the same. They give instructions to the computer. What the computer does will depend on the instructions given to it. Tell it to do something useful and it will. Give it instructions to perform a malicious task and it will do it without question. Even computers with artificial intelligence are simply following instructions that simulate human's way of thinking.

Computers do not care who gives the instructions. As long as the instructions are loaded into memory, the computer will process it accordingly. Upon startup, a short set of instructions will tell the computer to load and launch the operating system or OS. The OS in turn executes startup instructions that it finds. These include preparing the input and output drivers, as well as launching other background tasks. Having done that, the OS awaits command from its user to execute other applications.

Malware developers take advantage of these key concepts. They find vulnerabilities in the operating and network system that will allow them to install malware and have it running in the background. Vulnerabilities are bugs in the program that can let malware writers load additional code and execute it. These bugs or programming errors do not always appear during the testing stage.

Some malware writers use social engineering to trick victims into installing malware into their computers. They use the computer's connection to internal and external networks to propagate the malware. They infect shared storage to spread malware among colleagues. They hack into servers to install malicious code that will infect site visitors. They can do this because computers will run any executable code that is loaded into its memory.

What is Malware?

Malware is short for malicious software. It is a general term for a code that compromises a computer and instructs it to do malicious tasks, often without the knowledge or permission from the computer's owner. Early malware refers to programming challenges and pranks like programs that delete user files, but recent malware refers to targeting servers to make them inaccessible or for financial gains.

Home computers are not safe, either. Cybercriminals are using home computers to launch attacks on servers in addition to stealing personal information to access online bank accounts. Some advertisers adopt malware, too. They no longer wait for users to visit their sites, but install malware into a victim's computer so they can modify browser settings and change the default home page, eventually advertising their products every time a user opens the browser. They sometimes change the default search engine, replacing it with engines that track user habits to benefit advertisers.

Mobile devices are not safe, either. Today's mobile devices are computers with features and capabilities that are comparable to older computers. Mobile devices, like smartphones and tablets, are vulnerable because they require applications to work. If users inadvertently download a compromised application, then there is a possibility that malware can compromise their mobile devices, too.

A future malware playground is Internet of Things. It is a term for consumer devices like smart home appliances and vehicles loaded with small computers to provide intelligent functionality. These intelligent appliances connect to the Internet for remote control and administration. Having computers on these things, it may not be long until we can see malware on these devices too.

Remember that appliance manufacturers are not IT companies; hence, they may not have the capability to implement data security in their products. A hacker compromising a manufacturer's server could trigger a firmware update on connected appliances and make it perform additional functions, including attacking other servers on the Internet. It may sound like an event from a science-fiction movie, but this reality is possible.

What is the Difference Between a Malware and a Virus?

Many people confuse malware with viruses. A virus is a type of malware, while malware include viruses and other malicious software.

The first malware were viruses, and developers wrote antivirus software to eliminate these malicious programs. Even when viruses evolved to other forms, people still call them viruses and antivirus companies are using the same term even if they are targeting other malware variants.

Viruses are no longer common on their original form. With antivirus vendors constantly updating their algorithms, malware developers have to come up with new variants to avoid detection, often employing social engineering to propagate malware faster by tricking victims to install it along with legitimate software.

If we look at how malware developers remain active over the years, we can surmise that it is a financially rewarding business; therefore, we can expect cybercriminals to continue developing better malware while antivirus companies play catch-up. The only way to combat malware is to understand the threat it presents, how it spreads and propagates, how to detect it, and how to remove.

What are Potentially Unwanted Programs (PUPs)?

People love free software; however, developers need to earn money too. Malware developers see this as an opportunity to spread malware while providing revenue to free-software developers. What they come up with are installers for legitimate software that also install malware during installation. Antivirus companies call these Potentially Unwanted Programs instead of malware since victims give explicit permission to install them. They have no way of knowing if users allow the installation on purpose or unknowingly installs them.

Why would Users Give Permission to Install PUPs?

Most users do not bother reading user agreements that installers display during installation. Instead, they simply click on the default buttons or press enter. Even if users will read the agreements and prompts, some may not understand the message and assume that they are installing software that is necessary for the main program to work. Unfortunately, PUPs are easy to install, but are often frustrating to remove from the system. Most have more than one instance running such that removing a copy will trigger the second copy to re-install it. Many recent PUPs affect users' browsers, which can be very annoying.

How to Detect the Presence of Malware?

Users familiar with their computer will sometimes notice unusual behavior. Some are obvious, like the browser's looks suddenly changing. Other users may lose their files or the file types are changed. Users may even see system errors that were not present before.

Some changes are not visual, like a program accessing the hard disk and making noise even when the computer is idle. Malware accessing an external server can slow down Internet connection. Infected computers can also be unresponsive when hidden processes are running and using up the computer's memory.

Before assuming that malware may be causing the problem, try restarting the computer and leave it for a few minutes without running any program. If the computer is still slow, then there may be an unwanted background program running, but it still needs confirmation.

On Windows, check the hard disk space by opening any folder and clicking Computer on the left. A hard disk with very little space can slow down the computer and malware may not be the cause.

If there is plenty of hard disk space available, run the Task Manager by holding Ctrl+Alt+Del and selecting it from the menu. Click on the Performance tab and observe the real-time graph. Both the CPU and memory usage should be relatively flat if the computer is idle. An active graph could mean that a hidden program is busy. Click the Applications tab to confirm. There should be no application listed if the user did not execute a program. If there is no program listed and the CPU or memory graph is active then there could be a malware running in the background.

To see the process that is using up the memory, click on the Process tab, then click Memory to display the list in descending order. Check its Image name and description. Right-click on a name, then select Properties to get more details. Use a search engine to validate suspicious names.

The Networking tab can also give clues on the presence of malware. There should be no network activity if the computer is idle. If the network is slow and this graph is active, then a hidden program is accessing an external server or computer.

These are just some ways of detecting the possible presence of malware. Without knowing what the malware exactly is; however, it could be difficult to remove it manually.

Most leading antivirus software can detect and remove malware. For home users, there are free versions available that offer basic protection with the option to purchase upgrades for additional features.

A Note on USB flash drives

With the popularity of USB flash drives, spreading malware via USB is easier. Malware can automatically execute when the user opens a USB flash drive. Once in computer memory, inserting another USB drive will infect it. To prevent this, do not view the contents of a USB flash drive after it mounts. Instead, right-click on the drive's name or icon, then select the scan option from the antivirus. This will remove malware in the flash drive before using it.

If there are signs that a USB drive is infected, but the antivirus does not detect it, install another antivirus program. Some antivirus solutions are not good at detecting USB-based malware.

Antivirus solutions can prevent the installation of malware to some extent. However, there are malware that can still get through if the user is not aware of how they propagate. The best way to prevent malware from infecting computers is to understand how each type works.

The succeeding chapters give an insight into the various forms of malware. It also provides information on how they spread so that users can avoid infecting their computers. Prevention is still the best cure against malware. However, avoiding malware is not easy.

Chapter 2 – Virus

Viruses are the earliest forms of malware and they date back to the time before personal computers became popular. A virus is simply a program that can replicate itself on the same computer. Even without malicious intent, creating many copies of a virus code can quickly fill up the memory and slow the computer down. However, an unmodified virus cannot spread to other computers by itself even if the computers are on a network. Getting the virus inside a computer is the challenge for virus creators.

To avoid detection, virus creators modify legitimate programs by inserting malicious codes. When these programs launch, the virus loads into memory and scans the computer for other executable codes to infect. The virus code stays active in memory until the computer shuts down and the cycle starts again if the user runs the infected program.

Boot Sector Virus

Some viruses attack the boot sector of the computer's bootable disks. The boot sector is an area of a disk that a disk drive initially reads and loads into memory. It contains the startup code that will load other components of the operating system. When the boot sector is infected, the virus loads into memory every time the computer starts, ensuring that it is active without waiting for the user to run an infected program. Since the disk operating system can fit in diskettes in the early days of personal computers, starting a clean computer with an infected bootable diskette can also spread the virus to that computer.

Be Careful when Using Shared Resources

Viruses can spread through sharing. When a user mounts a removable storage media on an infected computer while a virus is active, the virus attempts to infect programs that it finds on the mounted media as well. In the early days, this applies to floppy diskettes and external hard drives, but infections are more common today on flash USB drives.

Once the user connects an infected storage to another computer and runs an infected program, the virus activates and infects the other programs in the new computer as well. This makes users who mount USB drives on shared computers at risk if the computer has no sufficient antivirus protection installed. For this reason, avoid connecting USB drives at Internet cafes and on other public computers.

Even shared documents can carry viruses. Some productivity software allows scripts or macros to automate common tasks. Scripts and macros are small, but powerful programs; hence, they can spread viruses, too. Executing an infected macro will also compromise other documents on the same computer. Worse, sending a copy of an infected document can also infect the receiver's computer.

Are Early Viruses Malicious?

Some early viruses started as programming challenges. There was a game that was named Core Wars where the objective is to create a program that loads in memory, then replicate and terminate other programs running on the same memory space. The competing programs create copies of the code while overwriting enemy codes to terminate them. The program that remains in control is the winner.

Other early versions are simply annoying. Two programmers wrote the Brain virus because users were illegally copying their diskettes. The Brain virus simply displays information about the programmers. The Brain virus spread to computers in other countries.

Computers were not widely connected before and the worst thing that a virus can do is to delete files or make them inaccessible. This is exactly what early destructive viruses did. Some programmers wrote viruses that display something interesting while deleting computer files.

Birth of Antivirus Companies

It was not long before other programmers started writing codes to remove viruses, turning the process into a never-ending game of cat and mouse. Virus creators are continually discovering new computer vulnerabilities that they can take advantage of, while antivirus developers update their codes to combat new virus strains. It has become a never ending battle between malware developers and antivirus companies.

Antivirus programs initially identify specific viruses using their signatures. Signatures are like patterns or fingerprints that identify specific viruses. Virus creators responded by continually creating virus variants that require new methods of detection to keep up. This is why antivirus programs update their databases almost daily.

Antivirus can only play catch up if they rely solely on signatures. Modern antivirus programs detect possible viruses by their behavior in addition to signatures.

Most free antivirus software in the market can eliminate common virus threats so not having one installed is not an excuse. While they retain the name, current antivirus software can detect and remove other forms of malware. To enable additional protection, users can purchase additional features.

However, those who do not have a budget for paid features can still protect themselves from malware. The key is to understand how other forms of malware spread. The next chapters will explain these.

Chapter 3 - Worms

While viruses were a threat due to their ability to replicate, it is not a tool for mass infection because it cannot spread to other computers. The capability to spread over the network by itself is a feature of worms. Networks include local area networks (LAN) that are commonly found in offices, Wide Area Network (WAN) for remote offices, as well as worldwide networks like the Internet.

Early worm research had good intentions and started as helpful ideas. One worm crawls networked computers at night to run processor-intensive tasks, but saves the work and stays idle during the day so people can use the computers normally. It is a good idea that maximizes computer resources, similar to how modern cloud computing works. However, a programming error caused the computers to crash and they had to write another program to remove it.

Another programmer wrote a seemingly harmless worm to check the size of the Internet. The worm creates copies on target computers as it moved from one computer to the next. Due to a programming decision, it can install a copy even if it already exists on the same computer. Multiple running copies of the same worm can slow down the computer until it eventually crashes. A single worm was able to crash a big part the Internet.

Worms spread across the network by exploiting operating system and application vulnerabilities and taking advantage of insufficient data security practices. Nowadays, worms can also spread through social engineering. Social engineering is a technique used by hackers to trick users into unknowingly breaking standard data security precautions. Hackers can bypass a highly secure environment using social engineering.

Operating systems, or OS, are programs that manage computers and network equipment. Just like any program, it can have unintentional bugs and updating usually fixes the problem. Worms take advantage of these vulnerabilities to compromise the system.

If the OS or application developer releases an update before someone announces the vulnerability, then users have time to update the operating system before a malware exploits the vulnerability. This is why users should install updates especially if the patch is to address data security issues. Allowing automatic updates usually takes care of this, although there is a risk of automatically installing buggy updates.

On the other hand, if a malware creator releases a worm before the developer discovers the bug and releases an update, what we have is zero-day vulnerability. Modern antivirus companies address this by developing algorithms that detect malicious behavior. However, very aggressive antivirus solutions may lead to false positives.

False positives result when a scan reports the presence of malicious code when there is none. A good antivirus has few false positives. Third party evaluations can determine effective antivirus solutions with fewer false positives.

Mass-mailer worms

Worms can access email clients on user computers and use it to email copies of the worm to contacts in the address book. Some of these emails can trick recipients into downloading and installing the attachment, compromising the receiver's computer in the process. When this happens, that computer also becomes a mass-mailing tool. Unfortunately, these worms can also get a name from the address book and change the From field with this name. This means that the sender in the email may not be the email source, making the source difficult to track.

Aside from possibly compromising recipients' computers, mass mailers can also slow down network performance. If a worm infects several computers on the same network, then it could eat up all the allocated bandwidth. Worse, data security companies may include the computer's IP address in the blacklist for spamming. This can affect all computers in the network that shares the same public IP.

This is because most offices and home networks use a single public IP address for their router while individual computers get private IP addresses. Worse, some DSL subscribers may get a banned public IP address when their router restarts.

Always be wary of unsolicited emails with attachment even if it comes from a trusted source. A possible indicator of spam mail is when the receiver's name is not mentioned in the salutation. Bad grammar is also a sign of possible spam email.

Do not assume that the antivirus can catch all worm variants. Some worms change the file extension of the attached file. Users may think that they are opening an image file when in reality they are executing a worm. Worms do this by adding a .jpg to the filename, like picture.jpg.exe. Since many users configure their computers to hide the file extension, they do not see that the real extension is .exe because the filename they see is picture.jpg.

Some mass-mailer worms simply send spam advertisements. While they may not do damage to a user's computer, they can still trick victims into purchasing illegitimate products. These emails often have a web beacon, a small image that is loaded from an external server. Displaying this image will send the user's email address to the server, thereby validating that it is an active email account. It will then be a target for future spam emails.

Note that spammers do not use their own computers to send mass emails. They use email worms to prevent authorities from easily tracking them.

Worms for Phishing

Mass-mailer worms provide a great platform for quickly distributing malware. Malware creators use these worms to transport different payloads depending on their intention. One application of mass-mailers is for phishing.

Phishing is a form of identity fraud and is usually for stealing personal information for financial gains. It works this way.

Malware creators will copy a legitimate website's looks, specifically the login and profile pages. Websites of financial institutions like banks and payment platforms are examples of these. Next, they will create an email that looks like an official document coming from the target institutions. These emails often have a sense of urgency, requiring the user to log in to the website immediately to validate or change the password for security purposes. It will also include a link to the appropriate page for the user's convenience.

There lies the trick. Instead of linking to the legitimate page, it will redirect the user to the fake login page after clicking the email link. The URL will have the legitimate website's domain name, but with added characters. Some users may mistakenly believe that they are in the genuine site and proceed to log in. After entering the login detail, the next page may even require them to enter their credit card details for validation.

In reality, users can enter anything in the login page and it will be successful. The login page will simply save the credentials entered by the user, then display a page to get other credentials. When in doubt, users can initially enter incorrect login credentials to check if the site can really validate their account. If it accepts a wrong username or password, then there is no validation and the site is a fake.

Another way to verify if a website is a fake is through browsing all the menus and internal links before entering the login details. Malware creators may not go through the trouble of recreating an entire website's content.

To guard against phishing, never click on an email link to log in or change account details. Always type the known URL on the browser address bar. If clicking an email link asks the user to log in, then do not continue. Instead, type the correct URL in the browser's address bar before logging in.

The next chapter discusses other payloads that worms usually bring.

Chapter 4 - Trojan Horse

Trojans are malware that disguise as useful programs or install together with a legitimate application. Its name comes from the Trojan War, a part of Greek mythology where a wooden gift horse had soldiers inside that attacked the enemies while they were asleep to win the war. Similarly, a Trojan pretends to be a useful application, waiting for the user to launch it to execute the malicious code. Once activated, trojans will run in the background to do their designated task.

Trojans do not replicate and spread by themselves. They often combine with worms to infect other computers. Trojans are also common on unsolicited email attachments, while some users download them along with valid applications.

There are several types of trojans according to function.

Root kits

Root kit is not inherently bad. It is originally a tool for system administrators. It becomes bad if the creator installs it on a computer without permission from the owner, especially if the purpose is to do malicious tasks.

Some trojans will modify the computer's system for hackers to gain access. Root kits are tools for administrators that hide in the operating system while providing a back door for their creator. With privileged access, a root kit's owner can do almost anything to the infected computer remotely. Root kits are good at hiding their existence, making them difficult to detect. They can also delete any traces of malware installation. Root kits usually remain hidden until activated.

Bots

Bots are programs that perform automated tasks. Some bots, called spambots, flood websites with spam advertisements to generate traffic for another website. This is common in online forums and is the main reason why websites validate users before accepting their registration details. Some registration forms require the user to type the characters shown on an image to validate that the applicant is human. However, some spammers go around this by hiring humans to solve the test, although it comes at a cost.

A more malicious bot is one that employs brute-force attack on target websites. Most website owners do not build websites from scratch, but simply use an open source Content Management System (CMS) as a starting point. A CMS is a fully functioning website that allows the user to update content without writing a single line of HTML code. There are many templates to choose from, and websites owners can customize further by using their own graphic images. Using CMS, owners can update website content in a few clicks.

Many CMS software have the default username "admin" and some website owners do not bother changing it. Given the default administrator name, hackers only need to guess the password to take over the website and install malicious software. If it is a popular forum, then there is a risk that hackers can steal the member database.

To attack a website, hackers write bots that log into the target website and try to log in with passwords taken from a table of common passwords as well as words from the dictionary. A website that does not limit failed logins in a given period is a good target. Using a network of zombie computers, hackers are able to brute-force attack a website using bots with minimal risk of authorities tracking the attack's mastermind.

Stolen password databases from forums are not safe, either. Using rainbow tables, hackers can use brute-force to find the matching password for a member account. Since many users employ the same username and password on all sites they register to, this allows the hackers to hack into members' accounts on other sites as well.

Remote-controlled Bots

Malware developers can turn an infected computer into a remote-controlled bot that will perform malicious tasks, including attacking another computer. This is how they get away with Distributed Denial of Service attacks. Attackers do not use their own computers to flood a server, but instead, they use a large network of zombie computers from unsuspecting users. This also saves the attacker from bandwidth costs since the computer owner is paying for it. It also makes it difficult to track the attacker after it spreads from one computer to another.

One analysis of an affected computer shows that bots log into a chat server, waiting for commands from its master. Think of an army of sleeper bots just waiting patiently for a command to attack. Developers will typically just let an installed Trojan do nothing until they have an army of remote-controlled bots to launch a large-scale cyber-attack. The attacker then issues the command to attack from the chat server where the bots log in each time the infected computer is running.

Without good anti-malware software, the presence of a remote-controlled bot in a computer is difficult to detect since it sleeps until a command is given.

Keylogger

Some trojans can capture keystrokes as well as mouse movements in the background without the user knowing it. Called keyloggers, these programs can serve as surveillance software for a good purpose. Some parents use it to monitor children's online activity.

Trojan keyloggers can steal passwords and other personal credentials from unsuspecting users. It can wait for specific events, like users opening a login page, before starting to record user actions and keystrokes. It then sends the log to a remote server for its master.

Spyware

Spyware is another Trojan that collects sensitive information similar to a keylogger. However, it is not limited to monitoring key strokes to steal user credentials, but can also gather information about the user's online activity as well.

Adware

Adware is similar to spyware, but simply records and sends users' online activity and behavior as marketing data to marketers so they can display an appropriate advertisement. Some versions will redirect browser searches to advertisements while others will replace the default search engine with an advertiser's search engine.

Adware creators write these malware for revenue generation. Adware that alters browser settings is very difficult to remove. Antivirus software can remove adware from the computer, but usually leaves the modified browser settings. Saving browser bookmarks and restoring to factory settings can sometimes fix the problem.

Ransomware

Ransomware does what its name suggests. After installing the malicious code, it will either prevent access to the infected computer or encrypt the contents of its hard disk. Users will see a message demanding payment to disable the malware. The criminals behind typically employ money transfer services that are difficult to track. Add this to the fact that these cybercriminals usually live in other countries, making it difficult to run after them.

To spread ransomware, cybercriminals typically take over a legitimate website, usually without the owner's knowledge, to install the malware. They can also spread ransomware using drive-by downloads on the compromised website.

Drive-by Download

A drive-by download will allow the installation of malware by simply browsing an infected website. The user does not even have to click a download link. The affected website contains codes that check for browser or operating system vulnerabilities that allow for automatic download. The malware will install a program with a task to connect to another server to download the rest of the malware. The victim may not notice the download due to the initial programs' small size.

Some anti-malware software can warn if a website has malware when a user tries to access it.

Suspicious Packers

In order to avoid detection, suspicious packers compress and encrypt malware code. Good anti-malware utilities are aware of this and are able to detect the behavior of suspicious packers and prevent them from executing.

Removing Trojans

Most antivirus companies have software that can automatically remove trojans. While it is possible to remove Trojans manually, this may be a challenge since many have multiple copies running that can reinstall copies if the user deletes one.

When looking for good antivirus software, try the demo versions first. If satisfied, users can pay for other features that provide complete protection to the computer. Some of these protections include email and web surfing security.

In some cases, antivirus software can remove malware from the system, but not from the browser. If removing browser add-ons and restoring to factory setting does not work, uninstall the browser and download again.

Avoiding Installer Trojans

Among the popular sources of Trojans are free software installers. Software development costs money, and offering it free is not good for business. However, many people would prefer free over paid versions, especially when performing simple or one-time tasks. To address this, developers break down their programs by specific features, then allow third party marketers to offer them as free downloads in return for revenue to the developer. For example, one utility can convert AVI formats to MP4, while another can convert MP4 to MPG.

How can marketers earn money from offering free downloads? They get revenue by offering their services to advertisers. These marketers create installers for legitimate software, then include the option to install software from other companies. There is nothing wrong with that right, except that many users do not bother reading what they are installing. Unfortunately, many of these optional programs are adware that antivirus software tag as Potential Unwanted Programs (PUP).

An installer for free software will first confirm that users want to install the desired legitimate program. After the user clicks on the Continue or Next button, the installer will get the user's consent to install additional software along with a few descriptions of its benefits. Sometimes, the installer will display an End User License Agreement (EULA), something that no one ever reads, but simply agrees to. It is common to see more than one program added in the installation. The problem, however, is that the default buttons will install these extra programs if the user is not careful.

How can users avoid these additional installations, especially if the user is unsure if the other software is required? Most installers have a Decline button for optional installations. When an installer shows the Decline button, then that additional software is probably a PUP. Pay attention to the presence of Decline buttons.

Some installers have no separate dialog boxes for additional software installation. Instead, easy and custom install options are available, with the easy install as the default. What the user may not see is that the easy install option will sometimes install additional software. Click the custom install option when it is available and deselect unfamiliar applications.

Some antivirus may give an alert that the installer has a Trojan. Always scan the installer after downloading. Users can do this by selecting the installer, right clicking then selecting the Scan option to run the antivirus. This is also a good practice after inserting USB devices.

Users can perform additional verification after each installation. In Windows, simply select Programs and Features from the control panel, then click the Installed On tab. Sort the list in descending order. The programs with the current date are the ones included in the installation. Select suspicious programs and click uninstall. To verify applications, enter the program name in a search engine to see what it does.

Chapter 5 – Threats on Mobile Devices

Mobile technology is now a part of people's everyday lives. Smartphones today are very powerful. They are no longer just for voice and text, but for accessing the Internet and playing games as well. Though not as efficient as personal computers, users can perform most tasks on their smartphones.

For those who require laptop capability at more portable form factor, tablets are a blessing. Those who want the small size of a phone, but with a bigger screen like a tablet, can choose a phablet. Mobile computing is now a reality.

As computers, these mobile devices can be targets of malware. To minimize these, Android and IOS, the leading mobile platforms, have screening policies in place to reduce the chances of malware getting into the official stores. Additionally, updates to the operating system often include security fixes for known vulnerabilities to strengthen the security of devices. Installing the latest updates, when available to the user's mobile device, addresses possible malware problems.

By default, users can only download apps from the official stores. This is Google Play for Android and App Store for IOS. However, a checkbox on Android's setting will allow the user to download from any external server. There lies the problem.

The price for mobile apps is quite low compared to their PC counterparts. However, many users still do not wish to pay for the apps they download, despite their low prices. Malware creators take advantage of this by making commercial apps available for free download on third party servers. By simply deselecting a default Android setting, users can now download a paid app for free.

Unfortunately, for them, these modified apps may contain malware written for mobile devices. Once installed on a mobile device and executed, these malware take over the device and do what PC malware often do. Some malware may steal user credentials while others may display unwanted advertisements. These malware can make the devices very slow, rendering them unusable. Restoring to factory settings may be the only option for some.

IOS has no checkbox to allow downloading of apps from unofficial sites, but bugs in the operating systems can allow jailbreaks. Jailbreaks are IOS hacks that allow users to customize their devices. It also allows users to install unofficial apps. Some of these apps may have malware and can compromise the device.

Malware creators are smart and can always find ways around a secure system. One company created a Windows application that allows users to download apps for free then transfer them to their IOS device. This comes with a risk, however, since some of these apps may also have malware.

Malware creators started targeting IOS developers in China. They did this by making local copies of Apple's development platform since downloading from Apple's official servers is quite slow for developers located in China. Unfortunately, the unofficial installer has malware that infects the apps they are developing. Some of these apps made their way into the App Store before they were discovered and removed.

Another malware creator took advantage of enterprise certificates. These certificates are used by companies to install their own apps on IOS devices without approval from Apple. Malware creators are tricking users to install an enterprise certificate so they can install apps with malware on victims' devices. Many users who do not understand the implications are at risk.

Apple quickly released an update to IOS that prevents this malware from installing. Those who are still using an older version of IOS can also avoid this malware by not allowing the installation of certificates unless it is from their company's IT department.

For IOS users, downloading apps only from the App Store can minimize the risk of malware. It does not mean that Android users are safer, though. Malware writers are invading Google Play by creating fake apps that mimic original apps, but with additional malware. Google has to monitor millions of apps and ensuring that apps do not have malware is not easy. There is a way to avoid potential malware, though. If an Android app asks for unnecessary permissions during installation, do not install it.

Fortunately, antivirus companies now have versions for both the IOS and Android platforms. Installing these apps will help users screen potential malware during installation, as well as remove malware that were accidentally installed.

Conclusion

Thank you again for purchasing this book!

I hope this book was able to help you understand malware threats to prevent them from spreading.

The next step is to check your computers for signs of malware and apply the lessons in this book to avoid infections in the future.

Finally, if you enjoyed this book, please take the time to share your thoughts and post a review on Amazon. It'd be greatly appreciated!

Thank you and good luck!

Book 2

Human-Computer Interaction

By Solis Tech

The Fundamentals Made Easy!

Table of Contents

Introduction

I want to thank you and congratulate you for purchasing the book, "Human-Computer Interaction: The Fundamentals Made Easy!"

This book contains proven steps and strategies on how to conceptualize and design a computer system that incorporate principles on effective interaction between the user and the device.

Human-computer interaction (HCI) is the study of the interaction between people and computers and the degree at which computers are developed enough to successfully interact with humans. So many institutions particularly academic and corporations now study HCI. Unfortunately, ease-of-use has not been a priority to most computer systems developer. The issue continues to bedevil the HCI community as accusations still abound that computer makers are still indifferent and are not making enough effort to make truly user-friendly products.

On the other hand, the designing task of computer system developers is not simple either as computers are very complex products. It is also true that the demand for use of computers have grown by leaps and bounds outstripping the need for ease-of-use by a significant margin. If you are a computer designer or simply have basic interest in making devices more effective for users, this book will help you a lot.

Thanks again for purchasing this book, I hope you enjoy it!

Chapter 1: Aspects of HCI

Main aspects of HCI

HCI is composed of three main features, namely: the user, the computer, and their interaction or how they work together.

"User" refers to either the individual or the group of users doing things together. An understanding of how the people's sense of sight, hearing, and touch send information is very important. Also, the type of mental models of interactions differs according to the personality of the user. And finally, interactions are also influenced by cultural and national differences.

"Computer," on the other hand, pertains to all technology from desktop to huge computer systems. As an example, if the topic is website design, the computer would then be the website. "Computers" would also include gadgets like mobile phones or even VCRs.

Finally, the "Interaction" is what happens as "User" uses the "Computer" to achieve a certain objective. Humans, of course, are totally different from machines. So the HCI's main intent is to ensure a successful interaction between the two.

In this aspect, adequate knowledge about humans and computers are critical to realize a functioning system. You need to seek inputs from users. Such knowledge would provide much needed information in determining schedule and budget that are crucial to the systems. In effect there are ideal situations and perfect systems. But the key is finding the balance between what is ideal and what is really feasible given the existing situation.

Objectives of HCI

HCI aims to come up with systems that are functional, usable, and safe. Developing computer systems with excellent usability depends on:

- having enough understanding of the aspects that lead people to use technology in certain ways
- being able to devise tools and ways for creating suitable systems
- the development of safe, effective, and efficient interaction

- making people the priority

The main philosophy underneath HCI is that the users or the people using the computers always come first. Developers must always be guided by the users' needs and preferences in designing systems. It is the system that should match the requirements of human users and not people changing to suit the nature of the machines.

The primacy of usability

Usability is one of the principal considerations in HCI. It is simply about ensuring that a system can be easily learned and used or be what is called user-friendly. A system is considered usable if it:

- can be learned easily
- can be remembered easily in terms of use
- is effective
- is efficient
- is safe
- is enjoyable

Lack of usability means wasted time, mistakes, and disappointments. Unfortunately, a lot of existing systems and devices have been designed without sufficient attention to usability. These include ATM, the Web, computer, printer, mobile phone, personal organizer, coffee machine, remote control, soft drink machine, ticket machine, photocopier, stereo, watch, video game, library information systems, and calculator.

A good example is the photocopier. If you are not familiar with the symbols on the buttons you will be greatly confused. For instance, the big button with the C on it actually refers to Clear, not Copy. The button used to produce copies is actually on the left side with an unrelated symbol. Devices and gadgets should be easy, effortless, and enjoyable to use.

Analyzing and designing a system based on HCI principles involve a lot of factors that produce really complex analysis because of interactions among many of them. The major factors are:

- <u>The User</u> – motivation, satisfaction, experience, enjoyment, personality. Also cognitive processes and capabilities

- User Interface – navigation, output devices, icons, commands, input devices, graphics, dialogue structures, user support, use of color, multimedia, natural language
- Environmental Factors – health and safety, noise, heating, lighting, ventilation
- Organization Factors – job design, work organization, training, roles, politics
- Task Factors – task allocation, skills, easy, novel, complex, monitoring
- Comfort Factors – seating, layout, equipment
- Constraints – budgets, buildings, cost, equipment, timescales, staff
- Productivity Factors – decrease costs, increase quality, increase innovation, increase output, decrease errors
- System Functionality – software, hardware, application

There are different disciplines representing a wide array of subjects that are covered in HCI. The manifold inputs from these fields have continued to enrich HCI. The disciplines include:

- Cognitive Psychology – limitations, performance predictions, information processing, cooperative working, capabilities
- Ergonomics – display readability, hardware design
- Computer Science – graphics, software design, prototyping tools, technology, User Interface Management Systems (UIMS) and User Interface Development Environments (UIDE)
- Social Psychology – social and organizational structures
- Engineering and Design – engineering principles, graphic designs
- Linguistics – natural language interfaces
- Philosophy, Sociology, and Anthropology – computer supported cooperative work (CSCW)
- Artificial Intelligence – intelligent software

Chapter 2: The Human Side in the HCI

Some of the key aspects that shed light on the human side of HCI are:

1. Perceptual-Motor Interaction. Effective human-computer interface design requires an appreciation of the whole human perceptual-motor system. The information-processing approach is central to the perceptual-motor behavior study and for considering the human factors in HCI. An effective interface design reflects the designer's knowledge of the perceptual such as visual displays, use of sound, and graphics. Also the cognitive exemplified by conceptual models and desktop metaphors as well as motoric constraints like ergonomic keyboards of the human perpetual-motor system.

   Man has gone beyond the use of computer punch cards and command-line interfaces. We now use speech recognition, eye-gaze control, and graphical user interfaces. The importance of various perceptual, cognitive, and motor constraints of the human system is now better recognized in HCI. An effective interface must take into account the perceptual and action expectations of users, the action that is seen with a response location, and the mapping of the perceptual-motor workspaces.

2. Human Information Processing. Aspects of human information processing such as models, theories, and methods are currently well developed. The available knowhow in this field is broadly useful to HCI in general such as in the representation and communication of knowledge and visual display design. An effective HCI requires making the interaction compatible with the human information-processing capabilities. Many things about human information processing have been integrated into cognitive architectures that are now applicable to HCI. These applications include the Model Human Processor, the Act model, the SOAR model, and the Epic model.

3. Mental Models in Human–Computer Interaction. Studying mental models can help understand HCI by inspecting the processes by which such models impact behavior. For example, mental models of machines can enable both novice and seasoned problem solvers to find new methods for fulfilling a task through more elaborate encoding of remembered methods.

   The Reverse Polish Notation is a great example of this. There is also a general theory that says readers develop a representation in their mind at several levels of what they read. First is the encoding of text, followed by the representation of propositional content of text. Finally, to this text, they integrate world knowledge to form a mental model of the situation described.

Readers also have the ability to look for ideas in multiple texts. They construct a kind of structured mental maps that show which documents contained which ideas even when they did not expect to need it while reading. Mental models are generally considered as semantic knowledge. Focusing on the degree of commonality among team members, for instance, when it comes to knowledge and beliefs, allows quantitative measures of similarity and differences which is the language of computers.

4. Emotion in Human–Computer Interaction. Emotion used to be persona non grata in the field of computer design. It had no place in the efficiency and rationality of computers which were the personification of zero emotion. Recent study findings in the field of psychology and technology show in a totally different light the relationship between humans, computers, and emotions.

   Emotion has ceased to be considered only in light of anger generated by inexplicable computer crashes or hyper excitement caused by video games. Nowadays, it is widely accepted that a host of emotions are important part of computer-related activities such as Web search, sending an email, online shopping, and playing computer games. In almost everything now, the emotional systems get engaged according to psychologists.

   Studies and discussions on emotion and computers have grown a lot because of dramatic advances in technology. Computers have actually been used to evaluate the relationship between emotion and its correlates. In the same vein, the astounding improvements in quality and speed of signal processing now enable computers to form conclusion on a user's emotional condition. Compared to purely textual interfaces that have very limited range, the multimodal interfaces that can use voices, faces, and bodies are now more capable to a broader range of emotions.

   Nowadays, the performance of an interface will be seriously impeded without considering the user's emotional state. Surprisingly, it can earn even descriptions like socially inept, incompetent, and cold. Much remains to be done to successfully incorporate emotion recognition into interfaces. Still, more studies about the interaction between design and testing can help create interfaces that are efficient and effective while providing satisfaction and enjoyment.

5. Cognitive Architecture. A cognitive architecture is a computer simulation program that makes use of human cognition principle based on human experimental data. It also refers to software artifacts developed by computer programmers. Likewise, the term also includes large software systems which are considered hard to develop and maintain.

Right now, cognitive architectures are not widely utilized by HCI practitioners. Nevertheless, it is quite relevant as an engineering field to usability and has important applications in computing systems especially in HCI. It also serves as theoretical science in human computer interaction studies. Finally, cognitive architectures combine artificial intelligence methods and knowledge with data and principles from cognitive psychology.

Presently-known cognitive architectures are undergoing improvements and are being utilized in HCI-related tasks. Two of the most well-known systems, EPIC and ACT, are production systems or built around one. All systems have production rules which differ from architecture to architecture. The difference lies on focus and history although there's a certain similarity in intellectual history. They may have more congruence than differences at some levels either because of mutual borrowings or due to the convergence of the science. The third system, Soar, is a bit different than the first two production system models.

The three production systems, Soar, Epic, and ACT-R were developed to present different types of human cognition but showed more similarities than divergence as they developed. It is not easy to describe a value possessed by architecture as advantage because to others it constitutes a disadvantage. For instance, Soar's learning mechanism is very important for modeling the improvement of users for a period of time. But there are many applications also where Soar's features result to harmful side effects that can cause more difficulty in model construction.

6. <u>Task Loading and Stress in HCI</u>. Stress in the form of task loading is central to HCI. The traditional perspective on stress sees it in light of exposure to some adverse environmental situations such as noise and the focus of attention centers on most affected physiological system. A new way of looking at it, however, stems from the findings that all stress effects are mediated through the brain.

   And since the brain is mainly focused on ongoing behavior or current task, stress ceases to be a peripheral issue but that the ongoing task becomes the primary source of stress. And this renders stress concerns that are central to all HCI issues. This means computer-based systems which aim at helping people lessen cognitive workload and task complexity actually impose more burdens and stress on them.

   The person's coping mechanism for such stress affects their work performance and personal wellbeing. The environment may vary but some mechanisms for appraising stress in all task demands are the same. So for HCI, certain principles and designs for stress are applicable across multiple domains.

There are several theories of stress and performance and their connection to human-computer interaction. Workload and stress are at times considered as varying perspectives on the same problem. There are some general practices for stress mitigation. But quite important for this topic is setting up effective measures of information processing and mental resources. It also includes expounding on task dimensions that are relevant and their relationship to self-regulatory mechanisms.

It is critical to establish how an individual's appraisal of his/her environment can be influenced by personal traits and states. This is because stress can only be understood vis-a-vis interaction between a person and the environment. Lastly, it is better to treat stress at multiple levels whether physiological or organizational when making practical application. Instead of one-dimensional which is bound to fail, multidimensional is better as it considers the person, task, and the physical, social and organizational environments.

The implication is that HCI researchers and practitioners should go beyond the design of interface displays and controls and focus also on the person aspects. What are the things in the individual that affect performance and the physical-social environment where the human-technology interaction happens? It means that the technical principles at work in that situation are not adequate. They cannot develop a complete description of the relationship between resources and cognitive activities.

7. <u>Motivating, Influencing, and Persuading Users</u>. From its former role as tool for scientists, the spread of computer use to all sectors of society has brought new uses for computers. Among those uses are persuading people to change their attitudes and behavior. Nowadays, it is widely accepted that skills in motivating and persuading people are necessary for developing a successful HCI.

   Interaction designers are actually agents of influence which unfortunately they have not yet understood and applied. Yet their works often involve creating something that tries to change people though they may not be conscious of it. Among these works are motivating people to register the software, learn an online application, or have product loyalty. Changing people's attitudes is now a common feature in the success of interactive products.

   Depending on the types of product, the persuasion factor can either be small or large. At any rate, anything that needs to be marketed needs to be persuasive. The growing use of computing products and the limitless scalability of software makes interaction designers one of the best potential change agents in the future.

Take for example the Web-interaction designers who increasingly are facing more challenge in designing something that will hold the attention and motivation of information seekers. After that, they need to persuade web users to adopt certain behaviors like:

- using a software
- joining a survey
- clicking on the ads
- returning often after bookmarking a site
- buying things online
- releasing personal information
- forming an online community

Being able to persuade people is a measure of success here. But with success comes responsibility. The Web designer needs to make the website credible. The following are some broad guidelines to ensure credibility:

1. Design websites to present the real and practical aspects of the organization.
2. Invest sufficiently in visual design
3. Make websites that people can easily use.
4. Include markers of good quality
5. Use markers of reliability.
6. Avoid too much commercialism on a website
7. Adopt and adjust to the user experience
8. Avoid being amateurish

To sum it all, computer systems have become an inescapable part of everyday life. The interactive experience involving all systems be it mobile phone or desktop can be designed in such a way as to influence the way we think and act. By combining the computing capability with persuasion psychology, computer systems can motivate and persuade. Humans are undoubtedly still superior when it comes to influencing people. But in many areas of endeavor, computer can do what humans cannot even imagine being capable of.

Computers don't sleep and can be designed to keep trying on and on. At the very least, computers provide a new way for modifying how people act and think. Like it or not, the community of HCI professionals is at the forefront of the campaign to make more sensitive and responsive tech products. It can rise to the challenge of helping churn out products that enhance the people's over-all quality of life. Or it can continue being a tool to produce mindless products whose main reason for being into is to make profit for the owners.

8. Human-Error Identification in Human–Computer Interaction. The leap from focusing on human error in technological problems to a less obvious culprit started in the 1940's. It was established during that year that plane pilot error was often designer error. It began to show that design is the key to

substantially reduce human error and this paradigm continued to gather steam particularly in HCI.

It is now common wisdom that human error can be as often as the product of a defective design or as a person making a mistake. The inadequate design fosters activities that lead to errors. A groundbreaking outcome of this new philosophy is that errors are now viewed as totally predictable events instead of seeing it as unpredictable occurrences. This makes errors avoidable.

So errors became instances where planned series of steps and activities fail to realize intended results independent of any outside change agencies. If errors are no longer random, then it can be identified and predicted ahead of time. What partially drove this line of thinking are the accidents that happened in the nuclear industry that is hungry for preemptive solutions. This has led to the formulation of several human-error identification (HEI) techniques.

Although evaluative and summative in nature, these HEI techniques that employ ergonomics methods can now be used in formative design stages especially in analytic prototyping. For instance, the entry of computer-aided design such as in architecture has profound impacts on prototyping. It made possible what was considered as impossible or too prohibitively costly design alteration at the structural prototyping stage.

The three main forms of prototyping human interfaces have been identified namely: functional analysis, scenario analysis, and structural analysis.

Functional analysis includes consideration of the functional range supported by the device. In comparison, scenario analysis is exemplified by consideration of the device in relation to events sequence. An example of the structural analysis, on the other hand, is the use of user-centered viewpoint in a non-destructive testing of the interface.

One compelling example of the crucial role of design in predicting and minimizing errors concern human error identification (HEI) tools like the TAFEI or Task Analysis for Error Identification. The results of the application of TAFEI on interface project designs show how it can improve systems and its relevance to other ergonomic methods. It served to validate what has been long suspected when it comes to error-design relationship as follow:

- Structured systems like TAFEI results to reliable and trustworthy error data;
- Most errors resulting from technology are totally predictable;

- To improve design and reduce errors, ergonomics methods should be employed in formative design process.

Exploring design weaknesses through tools like TAFEI will go a long way in developing and producing devices and gadgets that are tolerant to error.

Chapter 3: The Computer Side in the HCI

The salient points when it comes to the computer side in HCI include:

1. Input Technologies and Techniques. Input devices which are also a classification of computer can detect physical aspects of places, things, and, of course, people. However, its function is never complete without considering the visual feedback corresponding to the input. It is like using a writing instrument without something to write on. Input and output should always go together.

   And in devices with small screens, this is only possible with the help of integrated sensors. If the user or human characteristics are important in a maximized HCI environment, so are input technologies with enough sophistication to meet user-machine interaction requirements. Users can only achieve the task objectives by combining the right feedback with inputs. In this regard, the HCI designer should take into account the following:

a. the industrial and ergonomic design of the gadget

b. the physical censor

c. the relationship among all interaction techniques

Input gadgets have many properties that apply to the usual pointing devices or mobile items with touch input. These pointing devices include the: mice, trackballs, isometric joysticks, isotonic joysticks, indirect tablets, touchpads, touchscreens, and pen-operated devices. The mice or mouse, of course, is one of the most popular as anyone who has ever used a computer knows. Because of its inherent advantages for individual users where it can easily be used by most people, it is one of the most preferred pointing devices.

Touchpads are most well-known to laptop users. These are small tablets that are sensitive to touch and which are usually featured on laptop units. Touchscreens on the other hand are tablets that are sensitive to touch which are placed on a display. It is increasingly becoming the tool to beat because of the proliferation of smart phones and other hand-held devices.

There are input models and theories that are quite helpful in evaluating the efficacy of interaction strategies. But it would be most beneficial to readers here to focus on current and future trends for this feature. Interactive system designers should go beyond the usual things like graphical user interface and pointing ideas when it comes to inputs.

They must delve deeper into more effective search strategies, sensor inputs for new data types, and techniques of synthesis to make much better sense of data. Better search tools will enhance navigation and manual search regarding file systems. One outstanding development is the breakthrough in the development of more advanced sensor inputs such as technologies for tagging and location.

It allows computers to identify physical objects and locations that have been tagged, and to detect their location and distance to other devices through signal strength analysis. These sensors are making interface personalization much easier. This development in interaction also has great implications for data mining and techniques for machine learning. Continuous improvement in structure synthesis and extraction techniques is invaluable in this data-rich era.

An overriding aim in HCI is to achieve dramatic advancement in humanity's interaction with technology. The computer side of this presents limitless possibilities but the cognitive skills and senses of man will be relatively stagnant. Our holding, touching, and object-movement are not the result of technology-like progress but a product of our human limitations.

2. Recognition- and Sensor-Based Input for Interaction. Computers are able to manipulate physical signals that have been transformed by sensors into electrical signals. Sensors have found their way into various fields of industry such as robotics, automotive, and aerospace. It has also found vast applications in consumer products.

   The computer mouse is a very good example. Imagine that simple-looking device equipped with algorithms that process images and specialized camera that enables it to be unbelievably sensitive to motions. It detects movement at the rate of a thousand of an inch several thousand times per second. Another interesting device is the accelerometer that detects acceleration due to movement and continuous acceleration because of gravity.

   Digital cameras now make use of accelerometers to save a photo. Laptops also are equipped with accelerometers for self-protection. When the laptop is accidentally dropped the accelerometer enables the hard disk to secure the hard drive prior to impact. With smartphones, the goal is for motion sensing for the purpose of interaction such as determining the walking pattern of users. Generally, HCI research on sensors dwells on its usage to improve interaction.

   Sensor studies are either to broaden input options or build new computing forms. The new forms include mobile devices that recognize locations and places that are sensitive to the presence and needs of its inhabitants. Still there are far more advanced goals and applications like in robotics.

There is a race to develop machines that will behave and think like humans or at least complement their capabilities. It has many critical applications such as in nuclear power accident mitigation. One worry, of course, is that it will end up in the military. But in safety, mobile computing, entertainment, productivity, affective computing, and surveillance, sensors are finding widespread application.

An intriguing side note here is the idea of developing a sensor to enable computers to detect and accordingly react to the frustration of its user. The computer's response could be something like playing relaxing music. Sensing could be in the form of the user banging on the keyboard in frustration. A microphone could react to the yelling of the speaker or the webcam could sense scowling.

In general, the potential of interactive sensing is quite good. The degree of progress across the whole computing spectrum actually gives the impression that sky is the limit. Advances in nanotechnology, CPU power, and storage capacities will continue to produce more outstanding innovations in the computer side of HCI.

But what is driving the unprecedented growth of the sensor-based interactive systems is the dizzying expansion in devices outside the old desktop computer. It is hard to keep track of the explosive proliferation of smart phones, tablet PCs, portable gaming devices, music and movie players, living room-centric computers, and personal digital assistants. Computing is becoming part and parcel of our daily life and our environment.

Through recognition techniques and sensing systems, task-specific computing devices will be developed instead of general functions. It will also pave the way for different types of interaction style in HCI. This activity-specific interactive systems development will further hasten innovations on a much broader array of practical applications.

3. Visual Displays. Timekeeping has always been one function that man has strived for a good visual display. Today's smartwatches which are actually wrist computers sport stunning visual displays. It is no longer limited to displaying time but is multifunctional. Some brands can pinpoint exact location in the planet through a global positioning system. Others can show heart rate while a number can be personal digital assistants.

   The main idea behind wearable computing is that the human body is wearing the visual displays. One major way people use wearables is to put the display on one's head making user's hands free to work. It is called headmounted displays or HMDs. The screen-based is one category of HMDs. It makes use of the retinal-projection method which projects images on the retina of the eye.

An alternative method is the scanning displays which scan images onto the retina pixel by pixel. A second type of display which is actually much bigger in scope and the most widespread is the hand-held and wrist-worn displays. They are in mobile phones, media players, wristwatches, and other portable gadgets. Apple is one of the global leaders in this field and the most well-known. Even textiles for clothing are now being used for such technology in what is now known as photonic textiles-fabric.

Multicolored lighting systems were merged with the fabrics for its electronic information function without affecting the cloth's softness. It has sensors, GSM, and Bluetooth! Photonic fabrics have great promising applications in the areas of personal health care and communication.

4. Haptic Interfaces. Haptic interface refers to a device for sending feedback that produces sensation of weight, touch, rigidity, and other aspects through the skin and muscle. This force feedback mechanism is designed to enhance computer-human interaction. Because haptics are done through actual physical contact, they are not easy to synthesize unlike the sense of sight and sound that are gathered through the eyes and ears.

   The genius in the haptic interface is that it simply makes use of the body's own highly sophisticated receptor system. The haptic feedback is made possible through synthetic stimulation in the skin and proprioception.

   Proprioception involves something deeper than the skin – the muscle and skeleton. The mechanoreceptors in the body enable its detection of contact forces received from the environment. Body receptors sense velocity, skin stretching, vibration, and edges of objects. Haptic interfaces are more widely applied in the field of virtual reality than in information media and related devices are now available commercially.

Two of the most important research needs on haptic interfaces in the future concern the psychology in haptics and safety considerations. Safety is a crucial issue as insufficient actuator control can lead to injuries for users. Control problems may occur with the tool displays and exoskeleton. Unintended forces or vibration may pose danger to the user.

A locomotion interface that holds a user's body can cause serious physical damage if control is inadequate. It requires proven safety equipment that amply protects the walker and this should be a major objective of research. A much safer alternative is a system where the user does not wear any equipment during the interaction.

The psychology in haptics on the other hand requires more studies on muscle sensation as most existing findings are on skin sensation. Among the few promising findings relate to Laderman and Klatzky's work (1987) on force display and their recent study of forces distributed according to space. Their psychological findings have very promising applications in the development of haptic interface. A lot of obstacles need to be overcome before usage of haptic interface becomes widespread.

Though men cannot do without haptics in real life interaction, it is still of limited use in HCI. One can say haptic interface is still in infancy with its 10-year background. So eventually its time will come just like image displays (e.g. TV and movies) which started 100 years ago. For now, what are available are a few haptic interfaces with limited functionality and high cost. At the very least, haptic interface is a new very promising frontier in HCI with immense potential contribution to man's quality of life.

5. Non-speech Auditory Output. Sound is one of the key aspects that complete our interaction with our environment. But where speech is direct and necessitates focus and attention, non-speech sound is more diffused and provides a different class of information.

   Non-speech sounds include sounds from the environment, music, and sound effects. Nevertheless, speech and non-speech sounds complement each other just like text is complemented by visual symbols. Non-speech sounds can give information in a shorter period of time than speech.

   Right now, the non-speech field needs more research. The user interface is a much more effective tool for HCI when it employs a combined visual and sound feedback. This sound-visual combination has complementary function as well. Visual gives specific information about a small area reached by our eyes but sound or the auditory system provides more general information from beyond our focus.

   Our senses are the key to our effective interaction with the external world. These senses in turn bring more dimensions in information as they enhance one another. These principles are very useful in a multimodal HCI by adding non-speech sound output to the graphical displays. An example of this application is focusing our eyes on one task like editing a manuscript while monitoring other aspects in the machine through sound.

Reliance on visual sense which is more prevalent at present can be problematic. One problem is there could be visual overload which means the user could miss lots of information. Or simply that the viewer cannot look at everything at the same time at all times. Sound can help eliminate that situation by giving information to the user that the eyes could not see.

This interdependence between visual and audio could make information presentation far more efficient. Non-speech sound is mainly used in games' sound effects, music, and other multimedia usages. It is commonly employed in creating a certain mood for the item like in movies. In HCI, sound is used to provide information particularly those things that a user does not see or notice such as what is going on in their computer systems.

It is useful to use non-speech sound in HCI for many reasons. Seeing and hearing in the human body is first of all interdependent. The eyes can give information that is high-resolution only in a limited area of focus. But sounds can be received from all sides of the user: front, above, below, and behind. This not only provides direct information but also tells the eyes where to look to get more useful data. In fact, at times reaction to sound stimuli is faster than what is seen.

Non-speech sound can therefore help in reducing large display overload which can cause users to miss important data. This is especially true in large graphical interfaces that use multiple monitors. Using sound to present some information would reduce screen space. It would also lessen the volume of information that should be on the screen. This is most relevant to gadgets with small visual displays like smartphones and PDAs.

Non-speech sound would also decrease demands on our visual attention. For instance, a user who is walking would miss much information as he looks at his device's visual display because of competing attention from the traffic or uneven surface where he is walking. In fact, if the information is in sound, he does not have to look at his device at all.

Our sense of sound is also underutilized. Yet as exemplified by classical music, its intricate organization can make, say a symphony, a powerful tool for transmitting complex information. The beauty with sound is that it grabs attention. It is easy to avoid looking at something but hard to ignore sound which makes it very effective in sending important information. Likewise, certain things in the interface look more natural in sound than in sight.

Finally, non-speech sound will allow visually-impaired users to use computers. Newer graphical displays have, in particular, made it even harder for them to operate the device. Research has been extensive in the HCI application of non-speech sound in a wide range of topics.

There are two main areas of growth where the application of non-speech sound has the best potential. One is in the creation of multimodal displays that utilizes all available senses. This means integrating sound with other things like force-feedback and tactile apart from sight. The other area is in wearable and mobile computing gadgets that also use multimodal displays.

As mentioned, the screens of these devices are small and sound will reduce the need for screen space.

6. Network-Based Interaction. Networked interfaces have modified our perception of society and the world at large particularly with the Web and now mobile devices. There are several roles that networks play in HCI. The first is as an Enabler which refers to things that can be done only with network. The second is as Mediator which pertains to problems and issues caused by networks.

   Third is as Subject which focuses on managing and understanding networks and fourth as Platform which dwells on interface architectures and algorithms. Network includes both the wire-based and the wireless world. Things are rapidly changing especially in the wireless networks. These changes can be classified in two dimensions, namely:

   - **Global vs. Local** – refers to the distance by space between the connected points such as machines in the office to global networks like the Internet.

   - **Fixed vs. Flexible** – pertains to the nature of the links between points such as fixed devices and gadget that configures itself. More changes are coming because of spreading wireless links. One example is being able to gain access to internet connections and printers of another office by simply plugging a portable device into the Ethernet.

   Traditionally, LANs belong to local-fixed category while Internet is global-fixed. Hand-helds like cell phones are also categorized as global-fixed because phones are fixed and independent of location. The internet makes use of domain names which are fixed like URLs. Some phone technologies like GSM and GPRS are classified as global-fixed because it is possible to send content that is based on location. Also the enlarging data capability is enabling services to handle huge media content.

   What set these technologies apart, however, are the connectivity model and the charging which are usually by data use or fixed charge. There are a number of current and new technologies from the local-flexible type. These include the Wi-Fi, infrared, Bluetooth, and ZigBee which permit flexible connections among personal gadgets. With them, a computer device can utilize a mobile-phone modem or a headset with Bluetooth can make connections with a phone, wireless. Unfortunately, these capabilities also enhance unsavory activities like illegal equipment accessing, hacking, and surveillance.

7. Wearable Computers. Computers have become like appendage to many office workers. But it is hard for those using mobile devices to get the information

they need. In a mobile situation, existing interfaces will hamper the user's main task. Users will be forced to prioritize the device instead of the environment. The need is for a wearables design that helps fulfill not obstruct the task.

A framework that can be very useful in creating good designs of computer interfaces which are wearable is CAMP. This framework addresses different factors that may impinge on the effectiveness of the design such as body closeness and how it is used. CAMP stands for:

- Corporal – which means absence of discomfort to users during physical interface with the wearable.
- Attention – interface design should allow user to focus both on the real world and virtual reality.
- Manipulation – there are adequate controls which are easy to manipulate particularly in a mobile environment.
- Perception – Design must enable user to quickly perceive displays even when mobile. So displays should be easy to navigate and simple.

Outside offices and buildings, an attractive option for a user to have access to a computer interface is through wearables. There are challenges however that need to be addressed to fulfill the tasks in terms of contextual awareness, interface, adaptation to tasks, and cognitive model. These include:

- **Modalities of Input/output** – the ease of use and accuracy of modalities developed that try to copy the human brain's input/output capacity are not yet satisfactory. Frustrations bedevil users when there are inaccuracies. Also the computing requirement of these modalities is way beyond what low-weight wearable devices have. Input devices which are simple to use are needed.

- **Models of User interface** – there is a need for extensive experimentation in using applications involving end-users.

- **Capability-applications matching** – evaluation and design of interface should prioritize development of most effective way to access information and avoid creating additional features.

- **Simple methodology in interface evaluation** – current evaluation approaches are too complicated and time-consuming making them unsuitable in interface design. What is needed is an evaluation methodology that addresses frustration and human errors.

- **Context awareness** – for context aware computing to be realized, several questions must be answered. These include application models that integrate the social and cognitive aspects, social and cognitive mapping of inputs from many sensors, anticipating the needs of users, and interacting with the users.

Conclusion

Thank you again for purchasing this book!

I hope this book was able to help you to gain useful knowledge and understanding about human-computer interaction.

The next step is to apply what you have learned.

Finally, if you enjoyed this book, please take the time to share your thoughts and post a review on Amazon. It'd be greatly appreciated!

Thank you and good luck!

www.ingramcontent.com/pod-product-compliance
Lightning Source LLC
Chambersburg PA
CBHW060929050326
40689CB00013B/3018
* 9 7 8 1 5 2 3 8 6 7 0 3 5 *